POPULAR
SONGS

HAL LEONARD
STUDENT PIANO LIBRARY

T006137b

Sing to the King

Eight Modern Worship Songs for Piano Solo

Arranged by Phillip Keveren

CONTENTS

ISBN 978-1-4234-9002-9

HAL•LEONARD®
CORPORATION

7777 W. BLUEMOUND RD. P.O. BOX 13819 MILWAUKEE, WI 53213

Visit Hal Leonard Online at
www.halleonard.com

Amazing Grace

(My Chains Are Gone)

Words by John Newton
Traditional American Melody
Additional Words and Music by Chris Tomlin and Louie Giglio
Arranged by Phillip Keveren

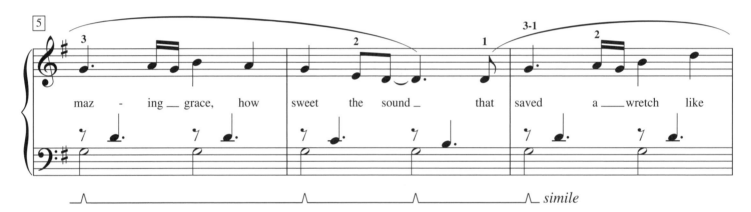

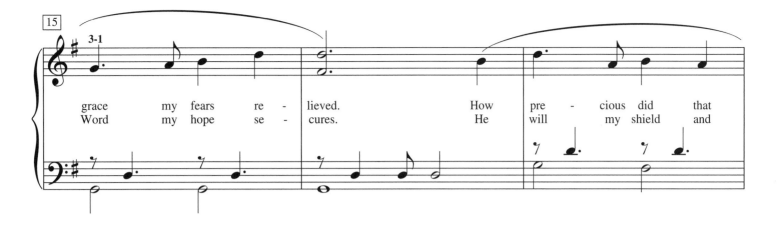

grace my fears re - lieved. How pre - cious did that
Word my hope se - cures. He will my shield and

grace ap - pear ___ the hour I first be - lieved.
por - tion be ___ as long as life en - dures.

My chains are

gone, ___ I've been set free. ___ My God, my Sav - ior ___ has ran - somed

me. ___ And like a flood, ___ His mer - cy rains ___ un - end - ing

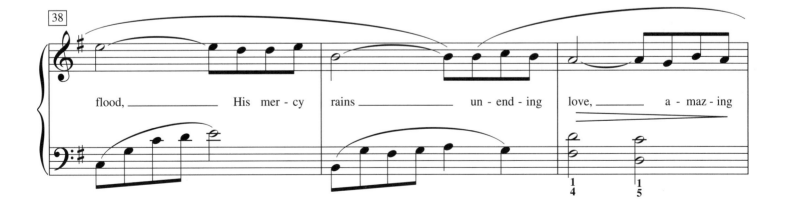

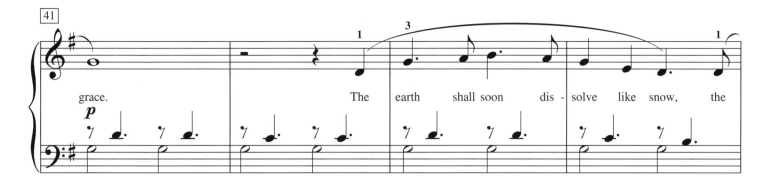

grace. The earth shall soon dis - solve like snow, the

p

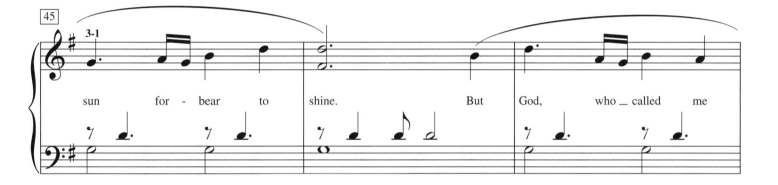

sun for - bear to shine. But God, who __ called me

here be - low, will be for - ev - er mine, will be for - ev - er

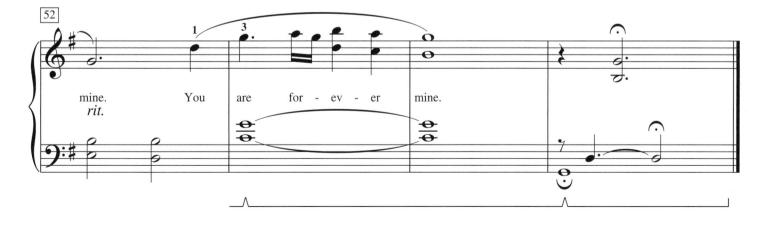

mine. You are for - ev - er mine.

rit.

By Our Love

Words and Music by
Christy Nockels
Arranged by Phillip Keveren

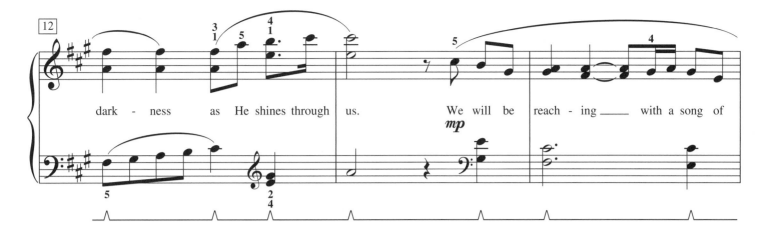

darkness as He shines through us. We will be reach - ing ___ with a song of

heal - ing, and they will know us by our love! The time is

now: come, Church, a - rise. Love with His hands, see with His

eyes. Bind it a - round you, ___ let it nev - er leave you,

and they will know us by our love!

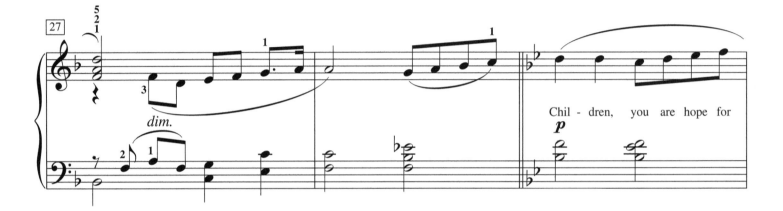

Chil - dren, you are hope for

jus - tice; stand firm in the Truth now, set your hearts a - bove. You will be

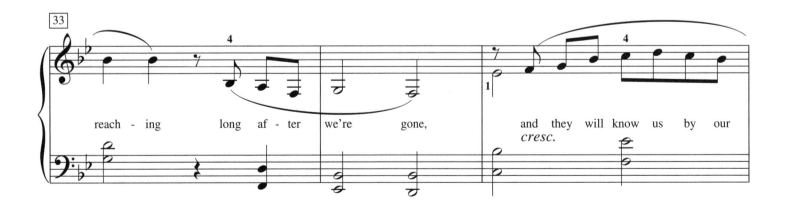

reach - ing long af - ter we're gone, and they will know us by our

love! The time is now: come, Church, a - rise. Love with His

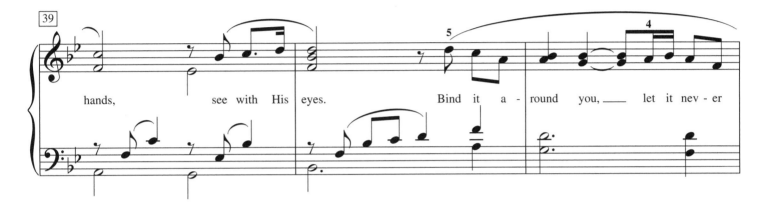

hands, see with His eyes. Bind it a - round you, ___ let it nev - er

leave you, and they will know us by our love.

And they will know us by our love.
molto rit.

R.H.

9

Everlasting God

Words and Music by Brenton Brown
and Ken Riley
Arranged by Phillip Keveren

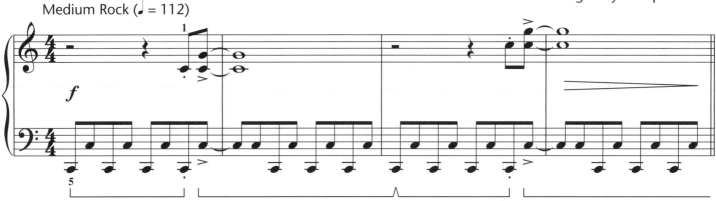

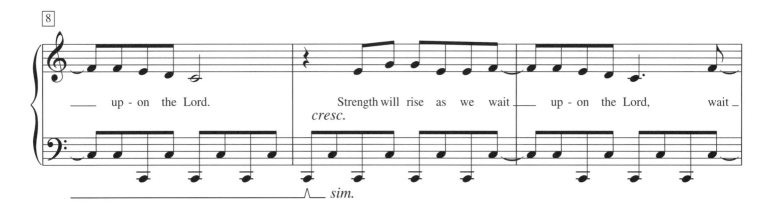

_____ for - ev _____ er. _____ Our Hope, _____ our strong _____

mp **cresc.**

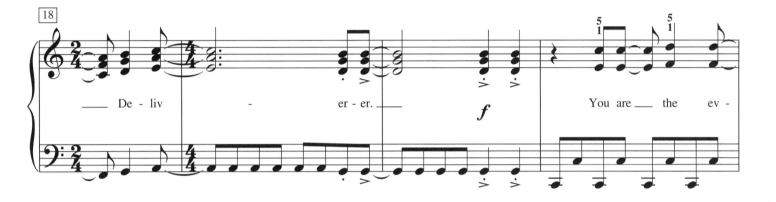

_____ De - liv _____ er - er. _____ You are _____ the ev -

f

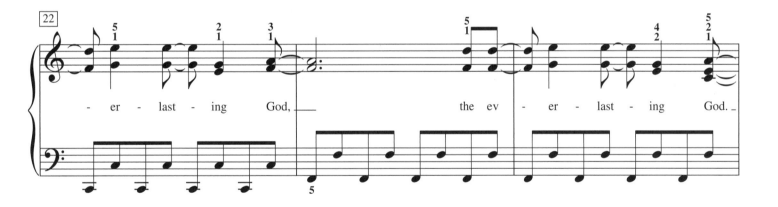

- er - last - ing God, _____ the ev - er - last - ing God.

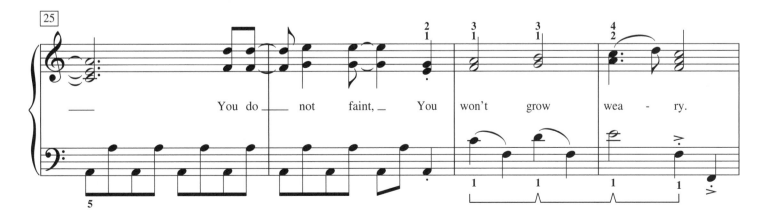

_____ You do _____ not faint, _____ You won't grow wea - ry.

You're the ___ de - fend - er of ___ the weak, ___ You com-

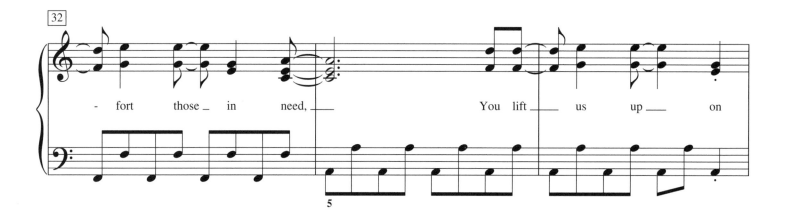

-fort those ___ in need, ___ You lift ___ us up ___ on

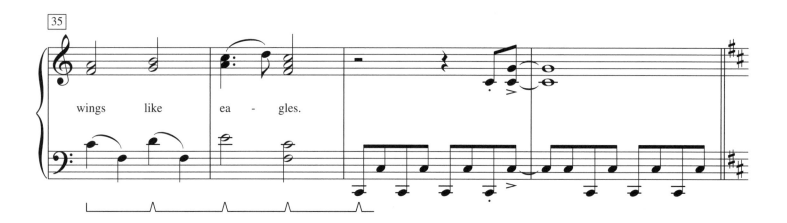

wings like ea - gles.

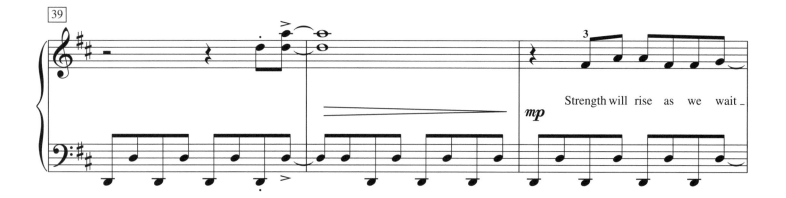

mp Strength will rise as we wait ___

up - on the Lord, wait up - on the Lord, we will wait up - on the Lord.

Strength will rise as we wait up - on the Lord, wait up - on the Lord, we will wait

cresc.

up - on the Lord. Our God, You reign for - ev -

f

3

- er. Our Hope, our strong De - liv -

mp   *cresc.*

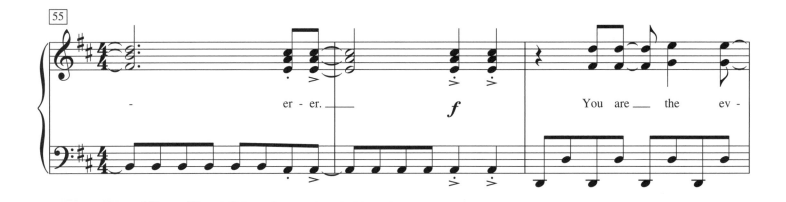

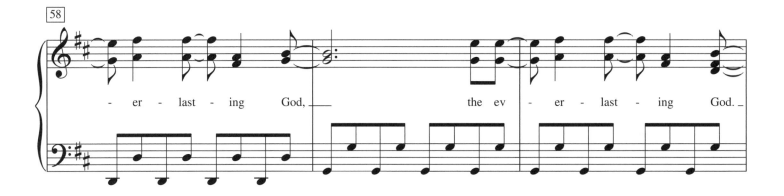

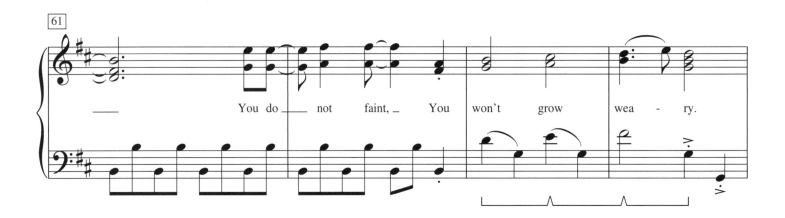

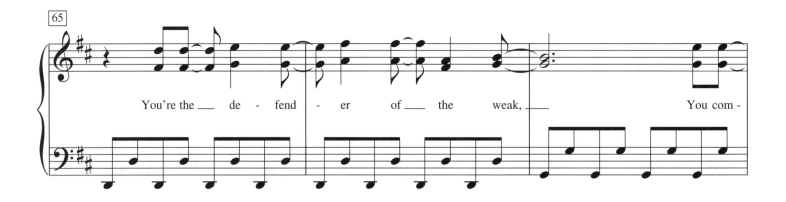

-fort those in need, You lift us up on

wings like ea - gles. *rit.*

p poco a poco cresc.
a tempo

ff

Revelation Song

Words and Music by
Jennie Lee Riddle
Arranged by Phillip Keveren

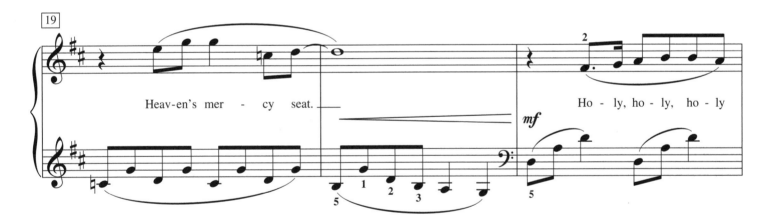

With all cre-a-tion I sing praise to the King of kings. You are my ev-'ry-thing, and

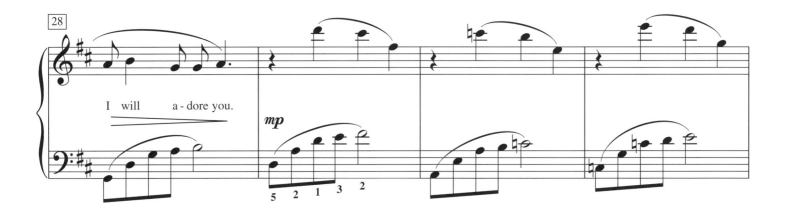

I will a-dore you. *mp*

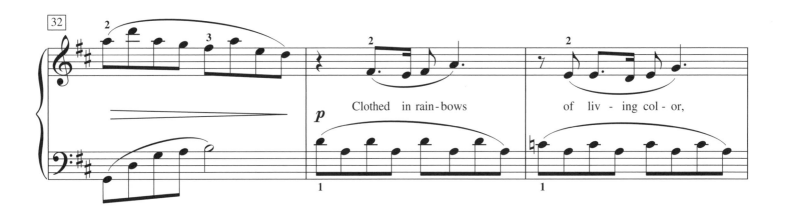

p Clothed in rain-bows of liv-ing col-or,

flash-es of light-ning, rolls of thun-der. _____ *mp* Bless-ing and hon - or, strength and

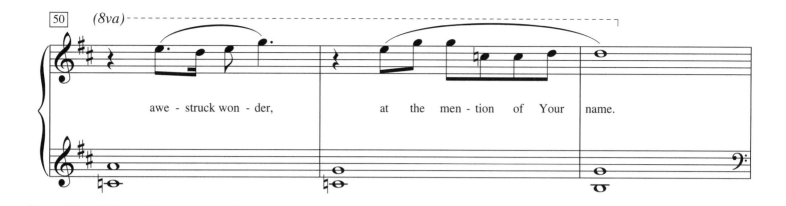

awe - struck won - der, at the men - tion of Your name.

mp Je - sus, Your name is pow - er, breath, and liv - ing wa - ter, such a mar - v'lous mys - ter -

y. *f* Ho - ly, ho - ly, ho - ly is the ___ Lord God Al-might- y,

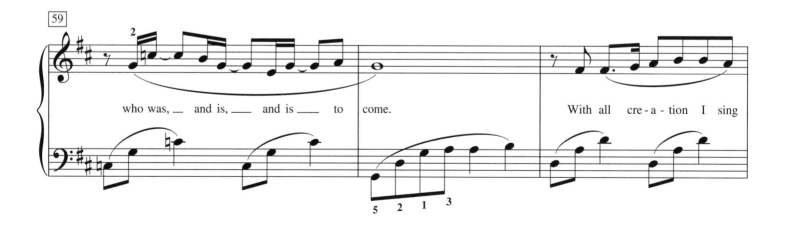

who was, ___ and is, ___ and is ___ to come. With all cre - a - tion I sing

praise to the King of kings. You are my ev - 'ry - thing, and I will a - dore you.

Ho - ly, ho - ly, ho - ly is the __ Lord God Al-might-y, who was, __ and is, __ and is __ to

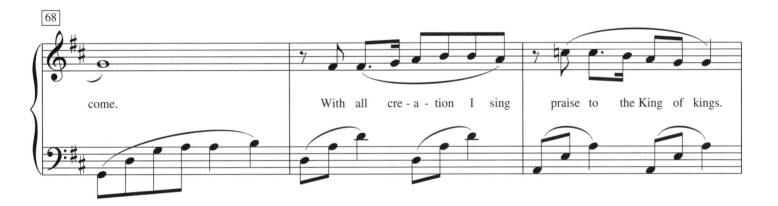

come. With all cre - a - tion I sing praise to the King of kings.

You are my ev - 'ry - thing, and I will a - dore you.

rit. e dim.

p

Sing to the King

Words and Music by
Billy James Foote
Arranged by Phillip Keveren

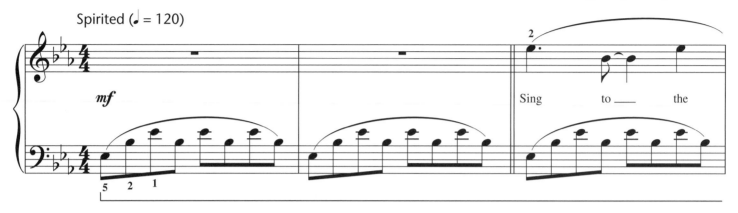

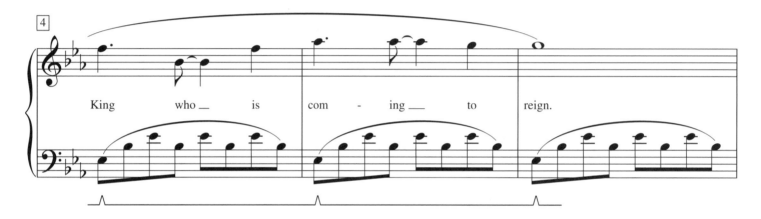

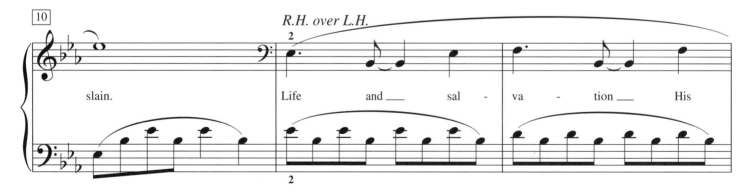

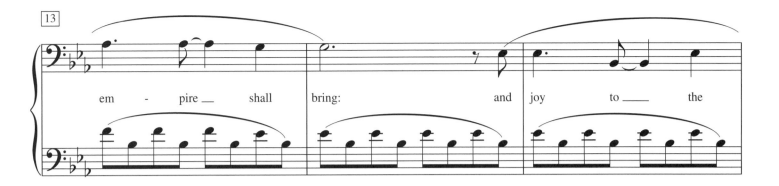

em - pire __ shall   bring: and   joy   to __ the

na - tions __ when   Je - sus __ is   King.

So   come,   let   us   sing __ a   song, __ a

song   de - clar - ing   we __ be - long __ to   Je - sus; __

23

and He's all __ we need.

Lift up a heart __ of praise, __ sing now with voic-

- es raised __ to Je - sus. __ Sing to __ the

King. For His __ re -

turn - ing __ we watch and __ we pray. We will __ be

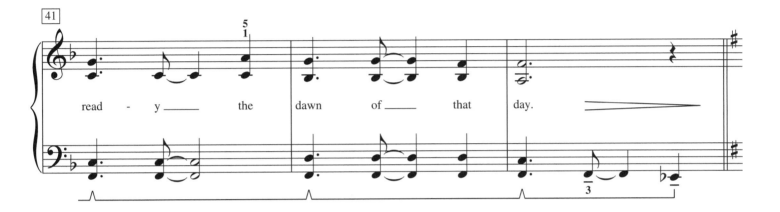

read - y __ the dawn of __ that day.

We'll join __ in sing - ing __ with all the __ re -

p cresc.

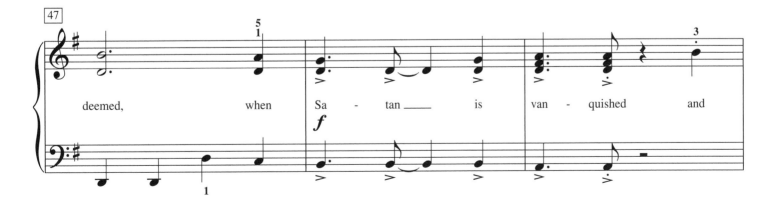

deemed, when Sa - tan __ is van - quished and

f

Je - sus is King!   So

come,   let us sing ___ a song, ___ a   song de - clar - ing we ___

___ be - long ___ to Je - sus; ___   and he's all ___ we

need.   Lift   up a heart ___

___ of praise, _ sing now with voic - es raised _ to Je -

\- sus. _____ Sing to ___ the King.

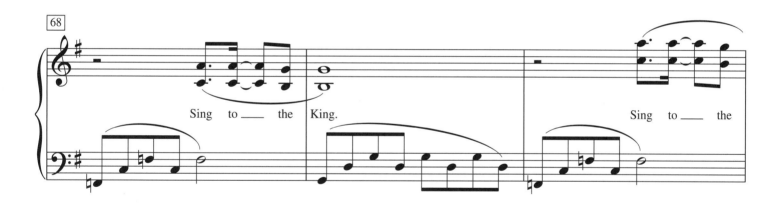

Sing to ___ the King. Sing to ___ the

King. *rit.* Sing to ___ the King.

Your Grace Is Enough

Words and Music by
Matt Maher
Arranged by Phillip Keveren

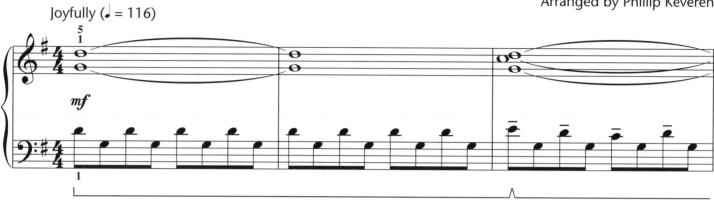

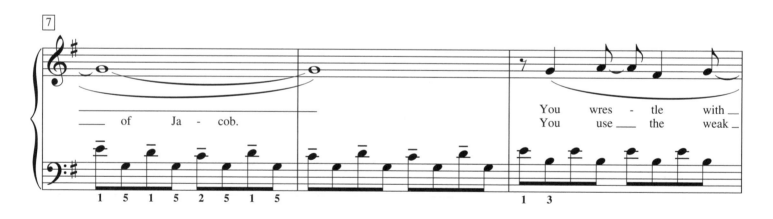

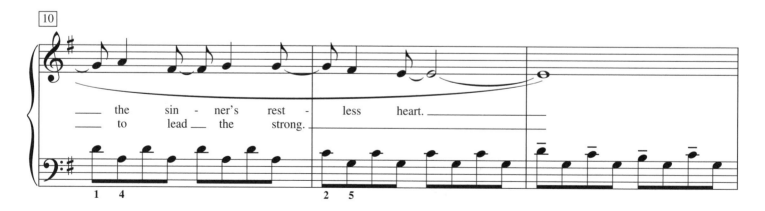

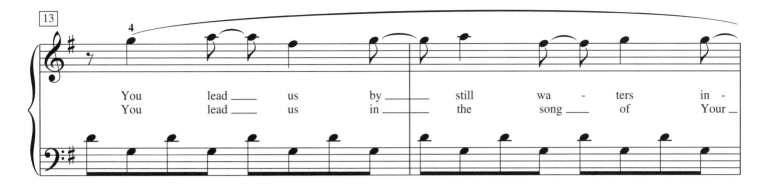

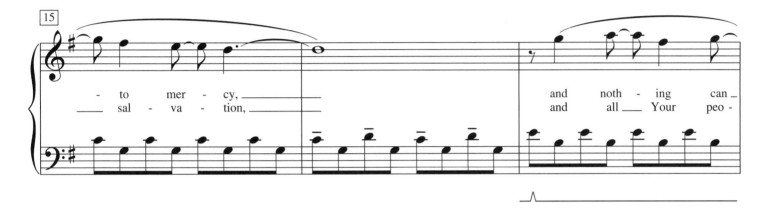

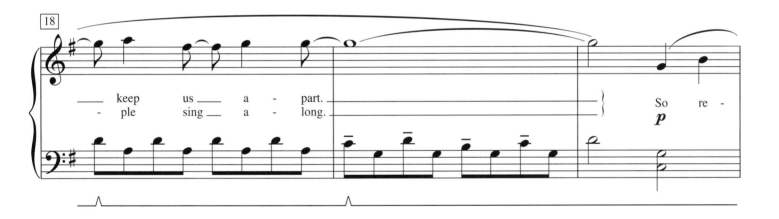

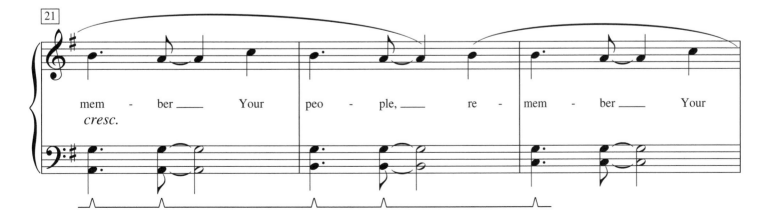

children, ___ re - mem - ber ___ Your prom - ise, ___ O

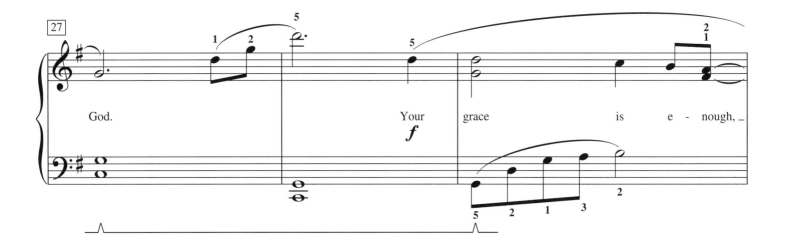

God. Your grace is e - nough, ___

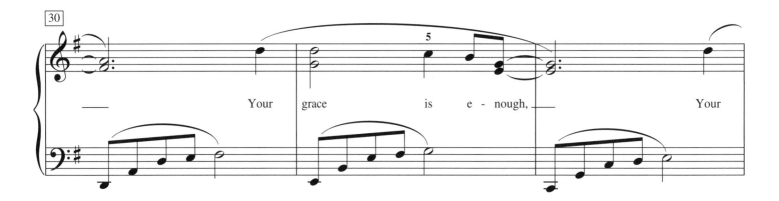

Your grace is e - nough, ___ Your

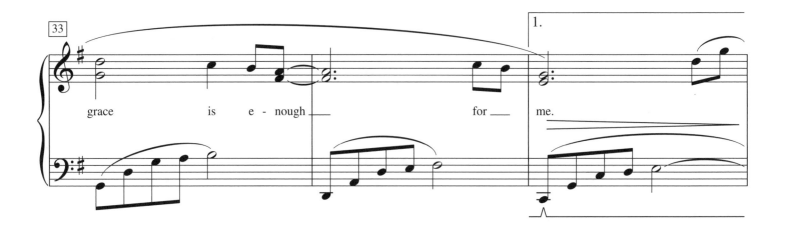

grace is e - nough ___ for ___ me.

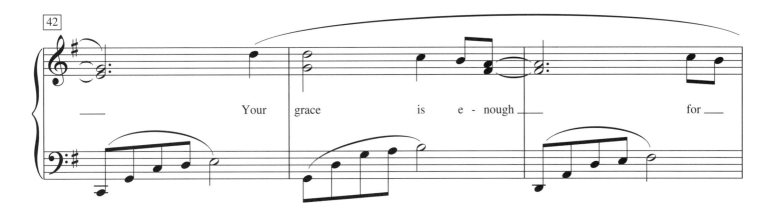

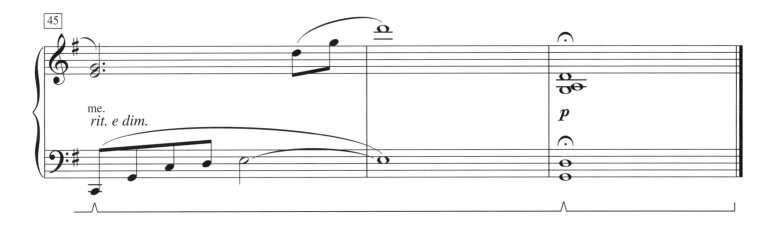

Your Name

Words and Music by Paul Baloche
and Glenn Packiam
Arranged by Phillip Keveren

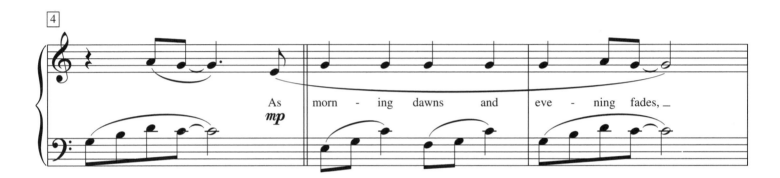

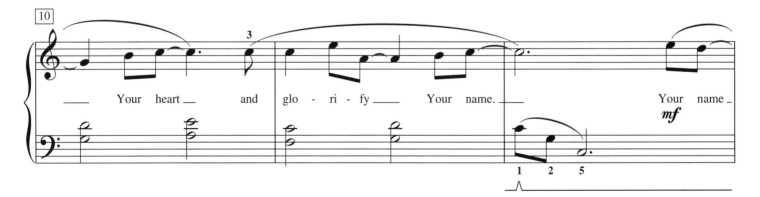

is a strong and might - y tow - er. Your name ____ is a

shel - ter like ___ no oth - er. Your name, ____ let the na - tions sing it loud - er, 'cause

noth - ing has the pow - er to save ___ but Your name.

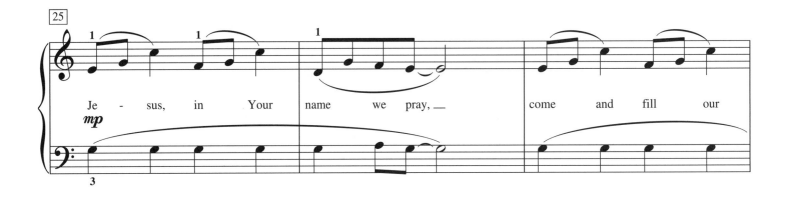

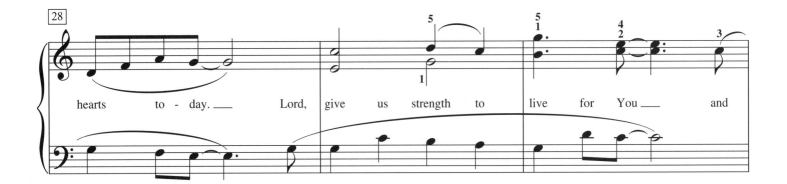

let the na-tions sing it loud - er, 'cause noth-ing has the pow - er to save

but Your name.

In Christ Alone

Words and Music by Keith Getty
and Stuart Townend
Arranged by Phillip Keveren

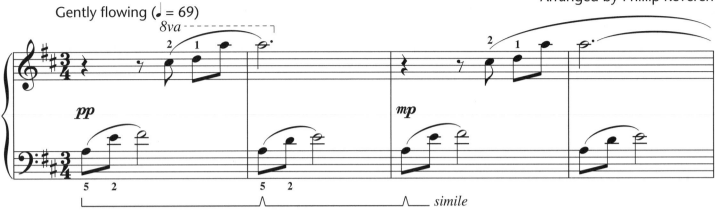

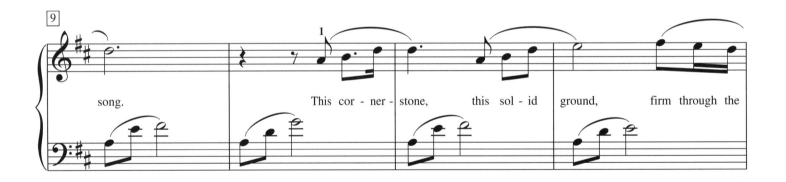

peace, when fears are stilled, when striv-ings cease! My Com-fort-

er, my All in All, here in the love of Christ I stand.

In Christ a - lone, who took on
ground His bod - y

flesh, full - ness of God in help - less babe! This gift of
lay, Light of the world by dark - ness slain. Then burst - ing

love   and right-eous - ness,   scorned by the ones He came to
forth   in glo - rious day,   up from the grave He rose a -

save.   Till on that cross   as Je - sus died,   the wrath of
gain!   And as He stands   in vic - to - ry,   sin's curse has

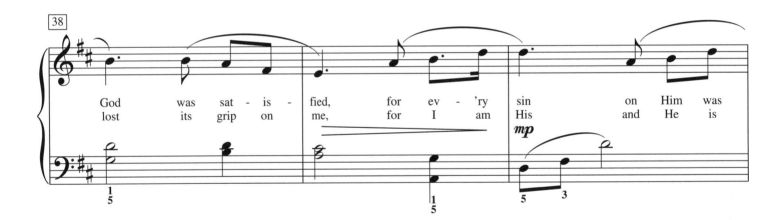

God   was sat - is - fied,   for ev - 'ry sin   on Him was
lost   its grip on me,   for I am His   and He is

laid;   here in the death of Christ I live.
mine,   bought with the pre-cious blood of Christ.

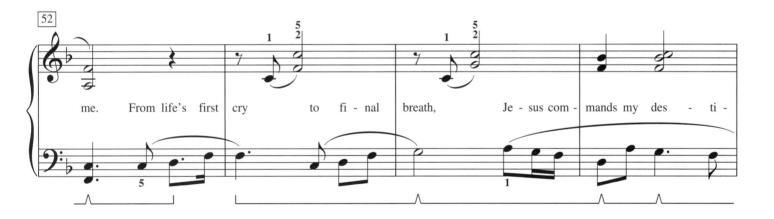

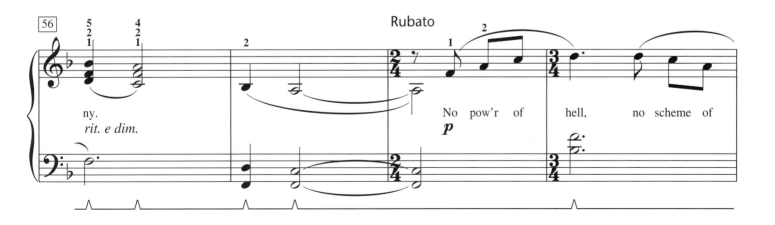

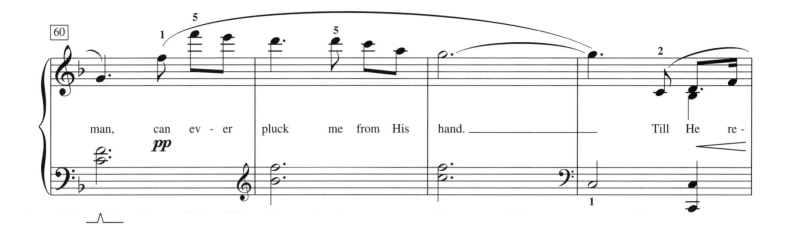

man, can ev - er pluck me from His hand. _____ Till He re -

Triumphantly (♩ = 60)

turns or calls me home, here in the pow'r of Christ _____ I'll

Tempo I

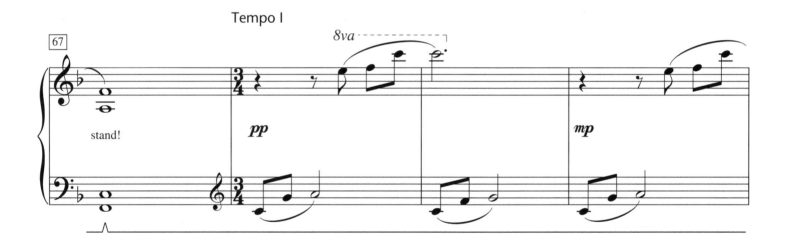

stand!